The Story of a Book

Written by Paul Reeder
Photographed by Greg Brookes

I can see you there reading me. I know you are looking at my pictures and reading my words. Do you know how I became a book?

First I was just an idea in someone's head. That person was my author.

2

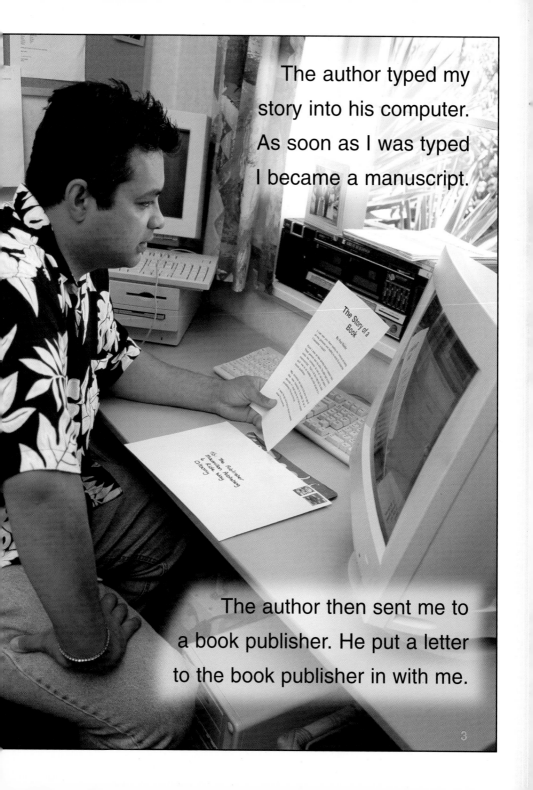

The author typed my story into his computer. As soon as I was typed I became a manuscript.

The author then sent me to a book publisher. He put a letter to the book publisher in with me.

When I got to the book publishers, I was read by a person who reads all the new manuscripts. She read me to see if they could make me into the kind of book they published. This was my first test.

I was the right kind of book, so I was sent to someone else for my next test.

The next person to read me
was the publisher. She is the person who
has the big plan about what will be published.

I passed this test too, so I was given to another person, called an editor.

The editor typed me into another computer. She changed some of my words and checked all my spelling.

Then the editor spread me out over some pages. She left room for my pictures. My pictures might be drawings or they might be photographs.

Next I was e-mailed to another computer. This computer had a designer working at it.

A designer is the person who puts the words and the pictures together to make the book look good.

The designer
and the editor talked
about my pictures. I was to
have photographs on my pages.

10

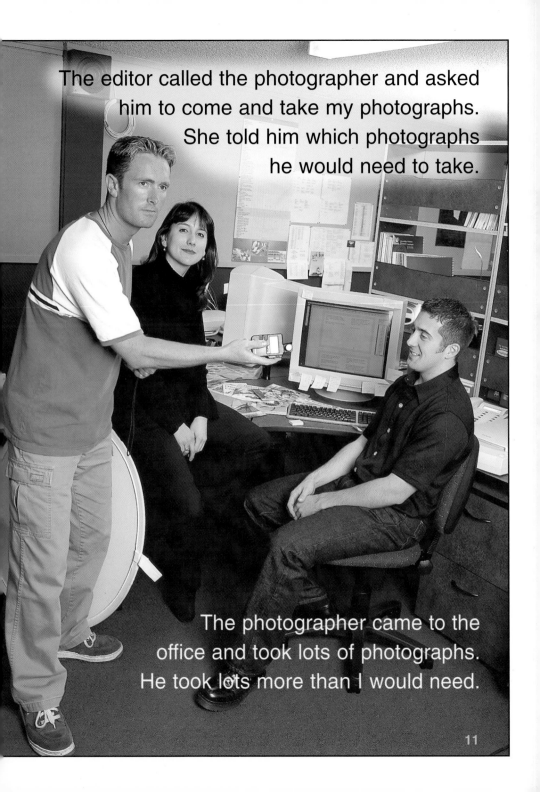

The editor called the photographer and asked him to come and take my photographs. She told him which photographs he would need to take.

The photographer came to the office and took lots of photographs. He took lots more than I would need.

When the photographs were ready, the editor and the designer chose which ones to use.

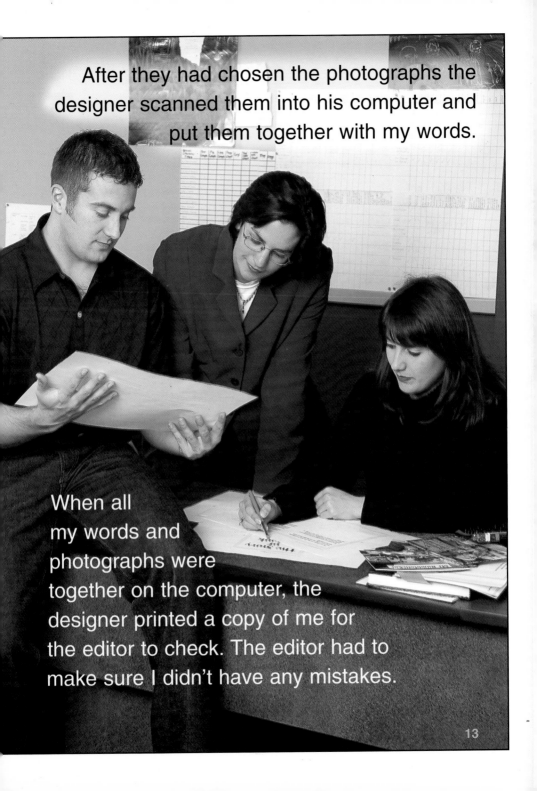

After they had chosen the photographs the designer scanned them into his computer and put them together with my words.

When all my words and photographs were together on the computer, the designer printed a copy of me for the editor to check. The editor had to make sure I didn't have any mistakes.

Then I was made into a little computer file and sent to another computer at a printing house. The printer made a film of me and used the film to make some printing plates.

The printing plates were put on a machine called a printing press. Then the printer added lots of inks to make all my photographs bright and clear.

The printer then put paper for my pages in another part of the press. Then the printer started the press and printed lots of copies of me onto big sheets of paper.

When the ink was dry, the big sheets of paper were sent to another machine. This machine folded and cut the big sheets into pages to fit into my cover. When they put my pages together with my cover, I became a book.

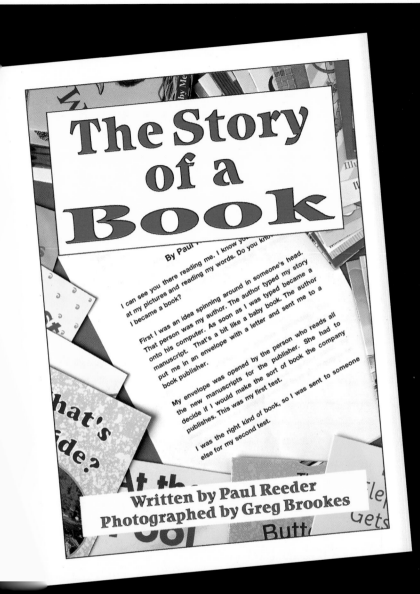

The Story of a Book

By Paul

I can see you there reading me. I know you are looking at my pictures and reading my words. Do you know how I became a book?

First I was an idea spinning around in someone's head. That person was my author. The author typed my story onto his computer. As soon as I was typed became a manuscript. That's a bit like a baby book. The author put me in an envelope with a letter and sent me to a book publisher.

My envelope was opened by the person who reads all the new manuscripts for the publisher. She had to decide if I would make the sort of book the company publishes. This was my first test.

I was the right kind of book, so I was sent to someone else for my second test.

Written by Paul Reeder
Photographed by Greg Brookes

Now you have read me,
you know the story of this book.

Glossary

An **author** is a person who writes something new, like a story, book or poem.

An **editor** helps turn a manuscript into a book, an editor checks the words in a book.

A **publisher** is the person who decides if a manuscript will be turned into a book.

A **designer** looks after the illustrations in a book and makes the book look good.

When something is **e-mailed**, it is sent from one computer to another computer.

A **manuscript** is the name for all the words and ideas for a book before it is printed.